VISION BOARD

CLIP ART BOOK

FOR BLACK WOMEN

VISION BOARD TIPS FOR LIFE-CHANGING MANIFESTATION

01 Be specific and clear about your goals and intentions, and choose images and affirmations that align with these intentions.

02 Select images that truly resonate with you and represent your desired outcomes. These images should evoke positive emotions and inspire you to take action towards achieving your goals.

03 Hang your board somewhere prominent where you will see it several times a day, e.g. by the kettle in the kitchen.

04 Incorporate positive affirmations that align with your intentions and goals. These affirmations should be uplifting and empowering, and should help to reinforce your positive mindset.

05 Every morning, choose one image, close your eyes and imagine how you will feel when it comes true. Transport yourself into the moment and allow yourself to feel like you have it already.

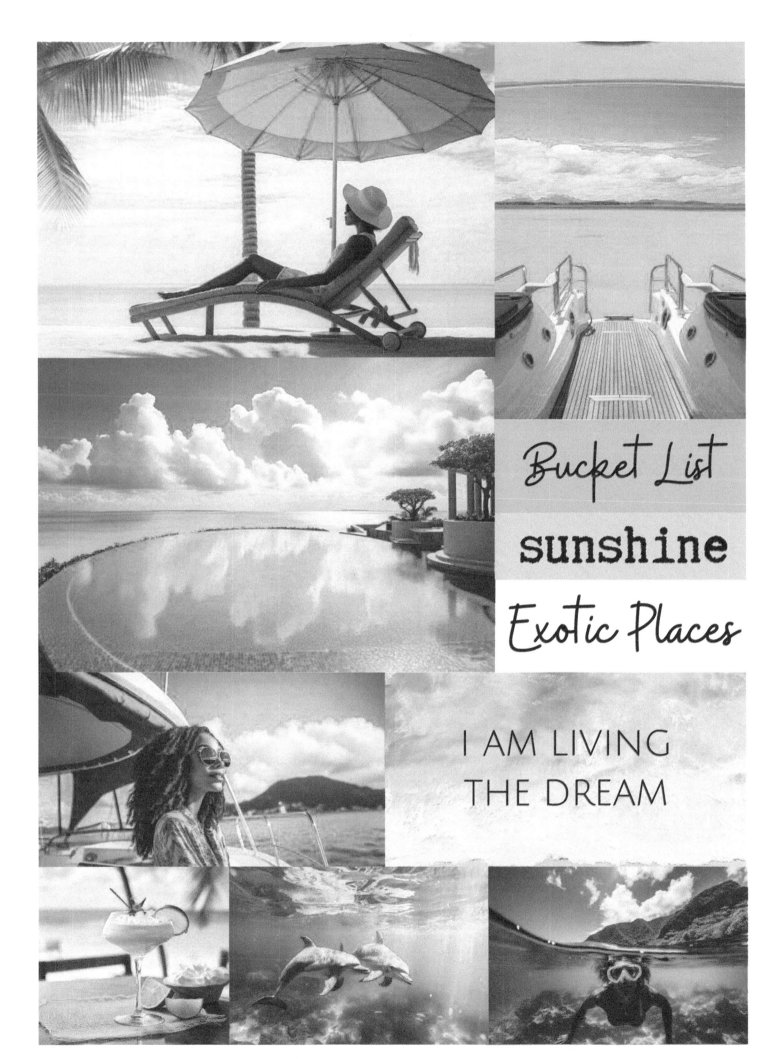

Bucket List

sunshine

Exotic Places

I AM LIVING
THE DREAM

Adventure

Vacation

TRAVEL

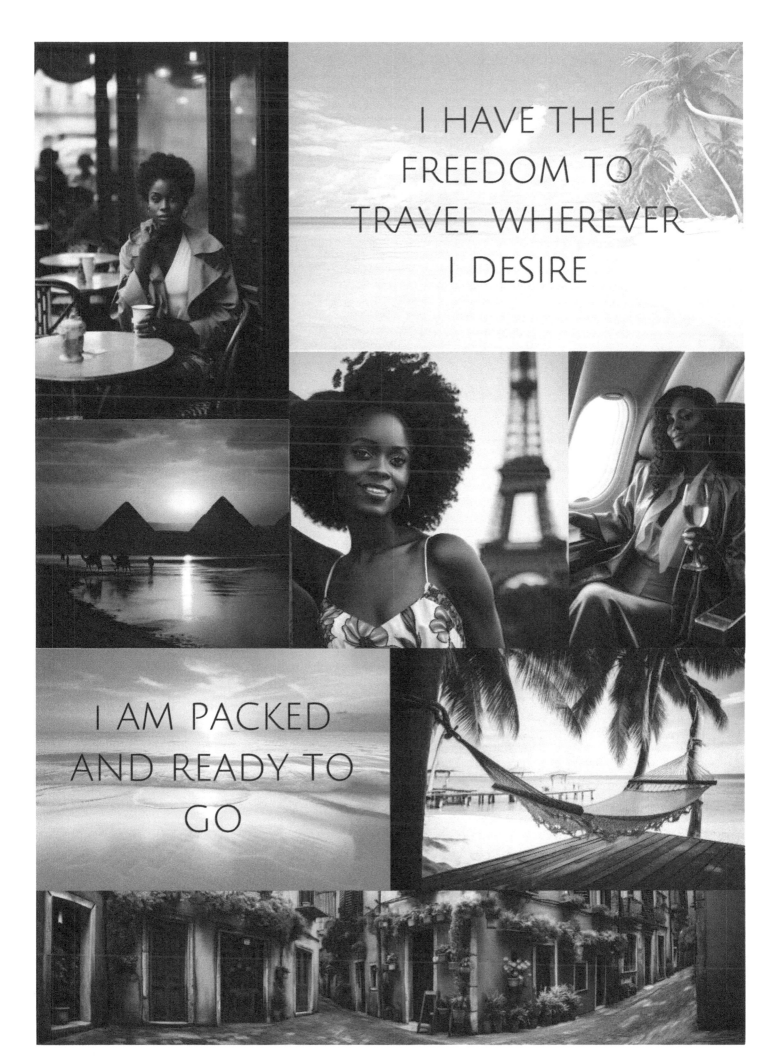

I HAVE THE FREEDOM TO TRAVEL WHEREVER I DESIRE

I AM PACKED AND READY TO GO

✈ UNIVERSAL AIRLINES

Boarding Pass

Boarding Pass

Passenger Name

Flight
AB 1234

Seat
15A

Passenger Name

From

Date

Gate
A5

From

To

To

Boarding Time
10:00 AM

Flight
AB 1234

Seat
15A

Gate
A5

0 1 2 3 4 5 6 7 8 9

Boarding Time
10:00 AM

✈ UNIVERSAL AIRLINES

Boarding Pass

Boarding Pass

Passenger Name

Flight
AB 1234

Seat
15A

Passenger Name

From

Date

Gate
A5

From

To

To

Boarding Time
10:00 AM

Flight
AB 1234

Seat
15A

Gate
A5

0 1 2 3 4 5 6 7 8 9

Boarding Time
10:00 AM

✈ UNIVERSAL AIRLINES

Boarding Pass

Boarding Pass

Passenger Name

Flight
AB 1234

Seat
15A

Passenger Name

From

Date

Gate
A5

From

To

To

Boarding Time
10:00 AM

Flight
AB 1234

Seat
15A

Gate
A5

0 1 2 3 4 5 6 7 8 9

Boarding Time
10:00 AM

✈ UNIVERSAL AIRLINES

Boarding Pass

Boarding Pass

Passenger Name

Flight
AB 1234

Seat
15A

Passenger Name

From

Date

Gate
A5

From

To

To

Boarding Time
10:00 AM

Flight
AB 1234

Seat
15A

Gate
A5

0 1 2 3 4 5 6 7 8 9

Boarding Time
10:00 AM

Miami

Sydney

Brazil

Tokyo

Greece

India

Italy

Maldives

South Africa

I'M ON MY WAY!

HELLO WORLD

Travel the world

Explore

Certificate of Graduation

awarded to

for

Date   Signature

DEGREE

boss babe

crushing it!

MASTERS

graduated!

I AM CAPABLE
OF WHATEVER I
SET MY MIND
TO

i did it!

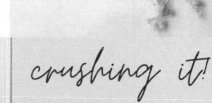

I embrace my authenticity

INFLUENCER

FOLLOWERS

Engagement

I create content that inspires, entertains & engages

BRANDING

ROLE MODEL

I get paid for being me

consistency

100K

positive mindset

Followers

I AM ATTRACTING A PARTNER WHO LOVES ME FOR WHO I AM

FIT

sexy

STRONG

PASSIONATE

kind

loving

HONEST

FUNNY

I AM EXCITED TO CREATE A BEAUTIFUL FUTURE WITH THE PARTNER OF MY DREAMS

my partner
is my best
friend

love

connection

SOULMATE

TRUST

DEVOTION

unity

intimacy

EMPATHY

MY HEART IS
OPEN, AND I
WELCOME
LOVE WITH
ARMS WIDE

wedding

engaged!

Mr & Mrs

commitment

YOU & ME

Certificate of Marriage

This Certifies that

_____ and _____

were united in marriage on

_____

MY MIND
AND BODY
ARE OPEN
AND READY
TO RECEIVE A
new life

I TRUST MY
BODY AND
IT'S ABILITY
TO
CONCEIVE A
healthy baby

GENERAL HOSPITAL

Certificate of Birth

This Certifies *that*_____

weight_____lbs._____oz. *was born in this Hospital*

on the _____ *day of*_____

In Witness Whereof *this Certificate has been
duly signed by the Happy Parents.*

_____
PARENTS

It's a boy!

It's a girl!

FAMILY: WHERE QUIRKS, CRAZINESS, AND UNCONDITIONAL LOVE COLLIDE

family time

blessings

forgiveness

Family - the ones who love you even when you're hangry

Family is like branches on a tree; we all grow in different directions, yet our roots remain as one

Lexus   Porsche

Mercedes Audi

Tesla   Volvo

BMW Range Rover

Pony

dog mom

meow

MY PET BRINGS
JOY AND LOVE
INTO MY LIFE

I am confident and successful

I AM EARNING LOTS OF MONEY DOING WHAT I LOVE

DREAM JOB

$ $ $ Payrise

TRUST THE PROCESS

CAREER →

Start your side hustle

MILLIONAIRE MINDSET

financial freedom

$$$

DEBT FREE

money magnet

I DESERVE
TO LIVE A
LIFE OF
LUXURY

I WAS
BORN TO
BE
RICH

I AM OPEN TO
RECEIVING
LARGE
AMOUNTS OF
MONEY

PROPERTY

investments

$1,000,000

WEALTH CONSTANTLY FLOWS INTO MY LIFE

luxury

DIOR

chanel

i don't
chase money;
it chases me

I ATTRACT
ABUNDANCE
AND WEALTH
INTO MY LIFE
EFFORTLESSLY

making
money is my
superpower

I'm not just in
the game; I'm the
game changer

RICH

INDEPENDENCE

fortune

GLAMOUR

BANK OF THE UNIVERSE

Date: _____

Pay: _____

_____ $ _____

_____ Dollars

The Universe

AUTHORIZED SIGNATURE

0123456 789 87654321   0123456 789 87654321

BANK OF THE UNIVERSE

Date: _____

Pay: _____

_____ $ _____

_____ Dollars

The Universe

AUTHORIZED SIGNATURE

0123456 789 87654321   0123456 789 87654321

BANK OF THE UNIVERSE

Date: _____

Pay: _____

_____ $ _____

_____ Dollars

The Universe

AUTHORIZED SIGNATURE

0123456 789 87654321   0123456 789 87654321

I'M EXCITED TO CREATE HAPPY MEMORIES IN MY *new home*

MY HOME IS FILLED WITH LOTS OF *love*

I FEEL SAFE IN MY *home*

dream home!

Romantic

RELAX ORGANIC

natural harmony

Boho Vibes

rustic CREATIVE

Peaceful

INNOVATIVE

LOFT STYLE

INDUSTRIAL

URBAN

METROPOLITAN

COUNTRY LIFE

Warm & Cozy

CANDLELIT BATHS

warm by the fire

homely

healthy

ATHLETE

exercise

Crushing it!

toned

energised

GLOWING

I GET STRONGER WITH EVERY WORKOUT

Spa Day

AS A BLACK WOMAN, I DESERVE THE BEST THINGS IN LIFE, AND I WILL NOT SETTLE FOR LESS

JUST
breathe

TIME TO
Relax

FOLLOW
YOUR
intuition

I
♥
MY LIFE

I ALLOW
MYSELF TO
feel
SO I CAN
heal

I MAKE
TIME FOR
myself

I EAT
NUTRITIOUS
FOOD

I AM
beautiful

DETOX

LOSE

POUNDS

FRIENDS FUEL MY SOUL

laugh louder,
love deeper

us against the world

shoulder to lean on

soul sisters

FRIENDS ARE THE
FAMILY WE
CHOOSE FOR
OURSELVES

companionship

sisterhood

by my side,

laughter

always

EMPOWERMENT

EDUCATION

LEADERSHIP

COMPASSION

RESILIENCE

WISDOM

CREATIVITY

SELF-EXPRESSION

DIGNITY

SUCCESS

INFLUENCE

GENEROSITY

AUTHENTICITY

SELF-BELIEF

COURAGE

DETERMINATION

INNOVATION

STRENGTH

God, show me how good it can get!

Love flows through me, emanates from me, resides in me and comes to me

I overcome every challenge set before me

I am blessed and highly melanated

Everything I need is within my reach

EMBRACE YOUR *uniqueness*

I AM BREAKING GENERATIONAL CURSES

I was created for this

I trust in the divine timing of my life, knowing that everything unfolds as it should.

"Therefore I tell you, whatever you ask for in prayer, believe that you have received it, and it will be yours."

- Mark 11:24

"Ask, and it will be given to you; seek, and you will find; knock, and it will be opened to you."

- Matthew 7:7

TREASURE LOVE Breathe

magic SOUL Spiritual

FOCUSED

magical I am strong read

Heal SHARING INTUITION

REST, RELAX CAREER My place

Weekend away self-care PEACE

RECHARGE THANKFUL Acceptance

Perspective FRIEND mighty

Eat well thrive FOREVER Soul

HEALTH Creative happier

FEELINGS I am enough SLEEP BETTER

DON'T STRESS Self-compassion TRUST

happiness

RITUALS

TRUE CALLING

Confidence

NEW DIRECTION

nurtured

visualise

pampering

move forward

transition

Meditation

Clarity

Hope

GOALS

WALK

POWERFUL

HEAL

HAPPY

self-compassion

CONFIDENT

positive

Learning

I am succeeding

I am loved

success

intimacy

New beginnings

ENERGY

Hey there!

We just wanted to take a moment to say thank you for choosing our vision board book. We hope it's helping you manifest your dreams and inspiring you to be the best version of yourself.

If you're loving the book, we'd be over the moon if you could leave us a review on Amazon. We love reading your feedback, and we appreciate it more than you know.

Also, we have other books that we think you'll love too! Check out our collection of Vision Board titles at www.amazon.com/author/gloriagreene, or scan this QR code.

Looking for even more images?

Subscribe to our newsletter and we'll send you EVEN MORE downloadable images AND a FREE eBook that teaches you how to use the power of positive thinking and visualization to manifest your goals and desires. Scan the code below!

FREE E-BOOK

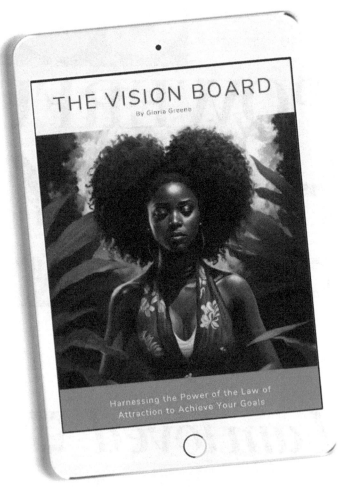

Scan this QR code to download your FREE downloadable images AND eBook.

Made in the USA
Las Vegas, NV
05 December 2023

82133304R00046